Since this book was first written, ~~many of our great Opry Stars~~ have passed away. This book, however, remains in the present tense so as not to change the original poems. Thankfully, the presence of these Stars will forever be with us.

GRAND
OLE
SATURDAY
NIGHTS

by
Margaret Britton Vaughn
Poet Laureate of Tennessee

BELL BUCKLE PRESS
P.O. Box 486, Bell Buckle, Tennessee 37020

Howdee!

"I'm just so proud" to say a few good words about this book of poems by my friend Maggi Vaughn.

There have been many folks who have loved the Grand Ole Opry and country music over the years. We value every one of them. But I doubt if anyone ever truly loved our music more than the talented author of this book. Her love shades and colors every line.

These poems are word pictures of the many facets of our country music – happy, sad, exciting, humorous phases of a unique art form which America cherishes and always will. Maggi has a way of expressing the feeling of both performer and listener. These poems are highly perceptive, sensitive, nostalgic, and yet up-to-date lyrics for the songs we wish we could sing.

You'll love the book. I do.

Sincerely,

Minnie Pearl

Dedicated
to
The Grand Ole Opry
and
those who have loved it

GRAND OLE SATURDAY NIGHTS

I've got all these years of Saturday nights
packed in an old memory.
I've been tucking them away for years
in a trunk as big as Tennessee.
There's been 500 tons of rhinestones
to shine upon my stage,
and I've seen enough cowboy boots
to stomp the Texas sage.
I've got enough broken strings
to tie up this whole world,
and I could build a mountain
out of names of inlaid pearl.
I've traveled enough miles
to go to some distant moon,
I've heard every lyric written
and I've sung every tune.
I've got stories that you've heard
that's been handed down for years.
I've got laughter to fill a hundred valleys
and three oceans full of tears.
I hold enough of your applause
to fill the outer space,
And seen enough curtains go up and down
to win any curtain race.
Yes, I've got all these Saturday nights
in this old trunk I'm rambling through,
and because you love me so much
I thought I'd share them with you.

OPRY BABY

I was born November 5, 1925
in a small WSM studio,
the first outfit I wore
was a fiddle and a bow.
The doctor that delivered me
was Dr. Humphrey Bates,
Uncle Dave Macon rocked my cradle
I remember this to date.
At first they called me Barn Dance,
that is, till I was two,
but then the Solemn Old Judge
gave me a name of new.
He nicknamed me Grand Ole Opry
and I've been called that ever since,
They thought I'd play in my backyard,
but soon I'd jumped the fence.
I wanted to see new places
with all my growing pains,
and I met and saw new faces
as I grew to fame.

Back then it didn't take a girl
too long to be grown,
and soon I'd be a mother
and have children of my own.
Lord, I was proud of Roy
when he became a star,
I brag on all my children
you know how mothers are.
Why, soon I had so many kids
I had to move from home to home,
then we moved into the Ryman
where we lived for so long.
No mother could be prouder
than of the family that I had.
And I'm still giving birth
at my age that ain't too bad.
I remember in 1932
down at the radio station,
they told me I was clear channel,
I was heard throughout the nation.
And then in 1939
Prince Albert visited me
and he stayed for years,
right here in Tennessee.
Oh, listen to me ramble
and all the stuff I said,
No wonder I'm getting old
and gray hair is on my head.
You know, here just lately
we had to move again,
we're in the biggest house yet
and it's something else, my friend.
I guess when you get up in age
things have to be more convenient,

I got air condition and more bathrooms
like none I've ever seen it.
So many people keep a comin'
every week there's a new face.
and with all these old timers coming back
we had to have more space.
But my family ain't changed at all
on that you can bet,
Roy still sings Wabash Cannonball,
Minnie Pearl ain't got married yet.
So you see I'm more comfortable
than I have ever been,
and who knows, maybe someday
I may have to move again.
But now I'm living on Briley Parkway
and I'm another year older this year,
so come to see us anytime
you're always welcome here.

Solemn Old Judge

Hank Snow

I REMEMBER

I remember one Saturday night
it was many years ago,
someone got tangled in the wires
I believe it was Hank Snow.
And I remember one night
the singer forgot his songs,
I can't remember who it was
but, I believe it was George Jones
And I remember one night
we laughed from all the fun,
I'm not sure but I believe
it was because of Faron Young.
I've got so much to remember
it kinda comes and goes,
it's so hard to keep straight
these many years of shows.

SATURDAY NIGHT

Now I don't like to boast
but you know that I'm right,
at one time I was all there was
to do on Saturday night.

IF

If you could take the heart of Doyle Wilburn
and the wit of Grandpa Jones.
If you could take the soul of Sonny James
wrap it around six feet of bones.
If you could take the mind of Chet Atkins
and a Marty Robbins grin,
roll them all into one
you'd have some man, my friend.

SOMEONE ASKED ME

Someone asked me what I'd been doing
now that all these years were down?
What would I be doing when
the next years rolled around?
Why, I'll be doing the same thing
as long as the wind blows,
goodness, when I'm five hundred
I'll still be doing country music shows!

JUST BECAUSE

Just because I'm older
and I'm getting gray hair,
don't think I'm a heading
for no old rocking chair.

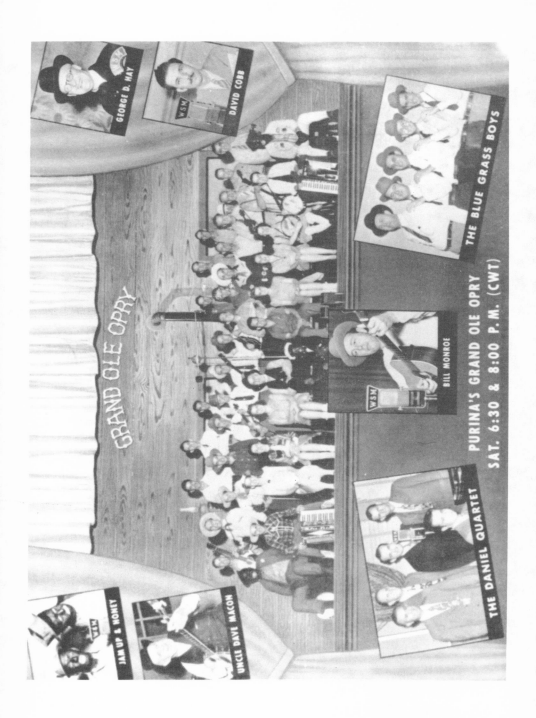

GRAND OLE OPRY

GEORGE D. HAY

WSM DAVID COBB

THE BLUE GRASS BOYS

WSM BILL MONROE

PURINA'S GRAND OLE OPRY
SAT. 6:30 & 8:00 P. M. (CWT)

THE DANIEL QUARTET

JAM UP & HONEY

UNCLE DAVE MACON

14

WORLD WAR II SHOWS

Wonder what ever happened to that old airplane
we used in World War II?
Lord, the shows we all put on
and the memories we went through.
We'd barely made it to the base
a minute to dress before the show,
then we'd be off for another place
another show to go.
But we made a million friends
in a time we were at war,
to have a friend – then be a friend
after all, that's what friends are for.

GRINDERS SWITCH

Last night I had a dream
and oh, how real it was,
I dreamed about Grinder's Switch
Minnie Pearl's Land of Oz.
And in this dream I had last night
I dreamed you were there too,
that is, all the ones Minnie loves
and that sure includes all of you.
Minnie taught us about simple things
like, how folk in Grinder's live
with Christmas Spirit all year long
not to receive, but to give.
We all spent the whole day
without one harsh word said,
and there was no talk of war
in the paper that we read.
We heard Uncle Nabob make
a statement clear and plain,
if people could get along in the hollows
looks like the Nations could do the same.
We spent the day without a worry
there they don't worry about a thing,
'cept what to name the baby
or if Sears catalog will be on time this Spring.

We saw a town full of love
a smile on every face,
a town that went to church on Sunday
and said a table grace.
And all of us became a part
of the town Minnie's known for years,
the place that grows the daisies on her hat
and waters them with happy tears.
And then a robin in a tree
woke me with his peep,
and I realized it was just a dream
that I'd shared with you in my sleep.
But Grinder's Switch is there all right
oh, not on a map or on a sign,
all you do is follow the path
that leads to peace of mind.
And I know that path is hard to find
and somedays it seems so far,
and sometimes because of our problems
we can't get there from where we are.
But I wish each one of you a Grinder's Switch
no matter how hopeless it may seem,
till then, I'll meet you this evening
same time, same place, same dream.

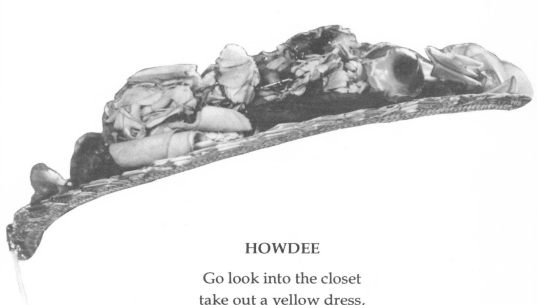

HOWDEE

Go look into the closet
take out a yellow dress,
then take a price tag hat
I think you know the rest.
Take one pair of black shoes
two white stockings above the knees,
put them all together
I'll be they'll say howdee.

The Gully Jumpers

CODE OF THE OPRY

There's a boy nineteen on my fifth row
he's got stars in his eyes,
he's listening to his favorite sing
the one he's idolized.
Got his first guitar when he was nine
that's when his dream began,
he would sing someday on my stage
sing with a country band.
He knows each and every song by heart
by bus, he's made the trip,
he's got a book of songs he's wrote
he knows will be a hit.
Keep on dreaming, son, that you're up there
cause someday you may be,
you see, they all shared that same dream too
that's the code of the Opry.

CHEWING GUM

Ryman, people left enough chewing gum
to outweigh a thousand cornfield ears.
No wonder you're still together
after all these years.

ROD BRASFIELD

Rod you were my little clown
you brought laughter to this world.
I can still see you now
joking with Cousin Minnie Pearl.
People still go though Hornwald
and ask about you,
They say did you know Rod
then they tell a joke or two.
So you still got them laughing
they remember your jokes still.
You were my little clown
I miss you Rod Brasfield.

Minnie Pearl and Rod Brasfield

THE BLUSH

What a blush you would have seen
here one Saturday night,
when Prince Albert decided to
kiss sweet Martha White.

TO THE D.J.'S

I recon if I had to pick someone
who's always stood by my side,
it would be the D.J. who
loved his music countryfied.
He's stood by us thick and thin
that's why we're where we are,
D.J. We applaud you
to us, you are the star.

THE FLOOD

That old river started rising
it came with the March wind,
and before it was all over
ole Opry learn to swim.

Bill Monroe

BLUEGRASS ALL THE TIME

In the fifties, they called it "hootnanny"
in the sixties, they called it "folk"
they thought they had something new,
found themselves a different stroke.
So we all sat around
and let them flip their mind,
on something they thought was new
but was Bluegrass all the time.

I WISH

I wish you could have been here
the night Ernest sang his first song.
Oh, but listen to me wish
that night has long been gone.
I wish you could have been here
the night Loretta lost her shoes,
or the night the lights grew dim
I nearly blew a fuse.
I wish you could have seen the night
T. Tommie lost his script,
and the nights so many forgot
the words to their latest hit.
I wish you could have been here
the night Cousin Jodie tried to dance,
or the night poor Stringbean
almost lost his pants.
I wish you could have been here
when Hank Locklin lost his place
or the night Barbara Mandrell
sang Amazing Grace.
I wish you could have seen the many things
that made this old heart prouder,
and Lord, I wished I'd taught
Bill Anderson to talk louder.

WAITING IN THE WING

There's a star at my microphone
excited and about to sing,
but he ain't half as excited
as the one waiting in the wing.
And that one you just clapped for
sure was a nervous thing,
but he ain't shaking half as bad
as that one standing in the wing.

SOMEWHERE

Somewhere there's an old backdrop
that I no longer need around,
somewhere there's an old microphone
that no longer can be found.
Somewhere there's an old script
that would be out of date today,
somewhere there's an old program
that someone stuck away.
Somewhere there in my memory
they all are in their place,
you see, a memory is one thing
that old time just can't erase.

BIRTHDAY PARTIES

I've had so many birthdays
blew out so many cakes,
got so many pretty presents
had so many handshakes.
The Crook Brothers gave me
a sweater one year,
Justin Tubb kissed me,
Stu Phillips called me "dear."

The Ralph Sloan Dancers
danced just for me one night,
Roy Drusky spanked me on his knee
boy, did I put up a fight!
The Glaser Brothers played a joke on me
and Bobby Lord helped them,
Hank Locklin and George Hamilton
just stood back and grinned.
Marion Worth sent me a telegram
Jim Ed Brown got me a puppy,
Jim and Jesse gave me a trip
I got a hug from Nat Stucky.
Archie Campbell drew me a picture
Ernie Ashworth sang me a song.
Del Reeves dropped the cake,
Bob Luman laughed all the way home.
Billy Walker gave me perfume
Jack Greene gave me a rose,
that brought tears to my eyes
so Charlie Walker blew my nose.
The Four Guys gave me candy
and the Osbornes ate it all,
Ray Pillow put me on his horse
and almost let me fall.
When you've got all those birthdays
and as many children as I do,
I'm glad it comes once a year
from the things that I go through.

Grandpa and Ramona

EIGHTEENTH PEW,
LEFTHAND SIDE

I'm the eighteenth pew, lefthand side
the stories I could tell.
They sat on me for hour on hour
I got to know them well.
There was a man from Tennessee
that weighed 300 pounds.
A group came in from Texas
I thought would tear me down.
There were newlyweds from Iowa
D.J.'s from Alabam,
one sang along on every song
the one from Birmingham.
Hand clappers, toe tappers, lap slappers,
by thousands they did come.
They sat on me happily
'til every song was sung.
The five year olds slept on me
and a few old ones too.
And the many nights I heard
"Mommy, I've lost a shoe."
Now there were those who saved for years
To fulfill their life dreams.
They came from corners everywhere
In furs and old blue jeans.
You're right, I've seen a bunch of them
in time, they all were here.
I'm the eighteenth pew, lefthand side
who got to know the rear.

Loretta Lynn

LORETTA
SING 'EM COUNTRY

Loretta, always sing 'em country
cause, that's what in you heart,
don't ever learn to talk up town
cause country's where you spark.

I'M THE SONG

I'm the song the farmer sang
while working his cotton field,
I'm the song that healed the heart
and made the sinner's kneel.
I'm the song that made them laugh,
I'm the song that made them cry.
I'm the song that said hello,
and the song that said good-bye.
I'm the song the soldiers carried
on to the battle ground.
I'm the song that brought the woman
to the other side of town.
I'm the song that millions sang
while rocking in their chair.
I'm the song called, our song,
that two people share.
I'm a song about the country
and about the city life.
A song about the hugs
a song about the fights.
I'm the song that will be around
for many years to come.
I'm the song that will be forgotten
before the setting sun.
I'm the song that said "I did"
and the song that said "I didn't."
But most important of all
I'm the song yet to be written.

MEMORIES IN GOLD

I cut my teeth on SPECKLED BIRD
raised on WABASH CANNONBALL,
spent my youth MOVING ON
to a plow boy's CATTLE CALL.
Educated me with CHEATING HEART
Lord, the things I've been through,
stayed awake one Saturday night
WALKING THE FLOOR OVER YOU.
When I was sixteen they picked
me a WILDWOOD FLOWER,
I've worn it all these years
will to my final hour.
I SAW THE LIGHT some years ago
realized I was grown,
ate all those CANDY KISSES
Till my hunger pains were GONE.
I went to sleep in DETROIT CITY
along with Billy Grammer,
UNCLE PEN kept me awake one night
I should have used a NINE POUND HAMMER.
Said YOU AIN'T WOMAN ENOUGH to take my place
but I guess I'm getting old,
just thought I would relive a few memories
that I helped make in gold.

Ernest and Justin Tubb

ERNEST TUBB

Ernest, at twelve on Saturday night
you became my pride and joy.
People will always think of you
as Nashville's midnight cowboy.

SADDEST MUSIC

Some say country music
is the saddest of all kind,
three beers and two Kitty Wells' songs
will make a man lose his mind.

JULY 4th

I can remember one hot night
July 4th was the date.
There was enough hand-fans going
to blow away New York State.

THE CARTERS

The spotlight came to center stage
an audience became wide eyed,
at home people waited to hear
that old radio by their side.
They knew it was that certain time
when Saturday night came about,
the Opry was at its best
when the Carter family stepped out.

THE FAN

He's saved his money all his life
so he could see me once or twice.
I know he grew up with me
though he lived far from Tennessee.
He's been true to me all these years
cause he's that kind of man,
God must have put aside a special day
to make a country music fan.

UNCLE JIMMY THOMPSON

Some won't remember Uncle Jimmy Thompson
cause he left us a long time ago.
But I can still remember one night
when Jimmy stole the show.
He fiddled for hours straight,
oh, you ought to heard him play.
And you wouldn't believe the telegrams
that came in the next day.
He had a smile on his face
as wide as his beard was long.
If Uncle Jimmy was still here
he'd still be fiddling on.

JIMMY DICKENS

Jimmy Dickens may be little
but it ain't because of fate.
It's because he had to always
take an old cold tater and wait.

Those participating in this Saturday night show
please sign here.

Tex Ritter

Rod Brasfield *Red Foley*

George D. Hay *Sallie*

Bill Monroe

Cowboy Copas

Patsy Cline

Uncle Dave

Jim Reeves

Roy Acuff

Minnie Pearl *Hank Williams*

Doyle Wilburn

Marty Robbins

Ernest Tubb

HEAVEN DELIGHT

Lord, you've got part of my family
up there with you,
by chance if they get on your nerves,
here's what you might do.
Give Hank a pen and paper
so he can write his songs,
send Uncle Dave to a country store
cause that's where he belongs.
Be sure Jimmy Thompson
has some rosin for his bow,
give Rod Brasfield some Southern jokes
cause Lord he talks so slow.
Let Patsy Cline sing for you
she'll warm your heart,
And if you want some harmony
give Ira Louvin the high part.
Give Hawkshaw and Copas a a big ole hat
and Jack Anglin a pretty tune,
and if you want to play cowboys,
ask for Tex around high noon.
Give Sallie some old bonnet
it meant more to her than gold,
And Lord help Stringbean find
one good old fishing hole.
If you could find a baseball
and pitch it to Jim Reeves,
Lonzo like baggy pants
that come just to his knees.
When Red Foley lost his dog
I guess we all wept,
so if you can see fit
let Red have back old Shep.
Doyle needs Mama Wilburn
to be by his side,
and you'll need one old bus
for Ernest Tubb to ride.

Red Sovine will want a truck
Marty Robbins a race car,
if you can stand the smoke
give Archie a cigar.
Be sure there's an old upright
tuned up for Del,
"Down Yonder," stands for Dixie
it don't stand for Hell.
Make sure the Carter's are united
Mother Maybelle came that way,
George Morgan loves candy kisses
he eats them night and day.
Grow a lot of Bluegrass
for Kentucky's Bill Monroe.
Dottie West needs lots of sunshine
Judge Hay, a horn to blow.
That train that pulled in
was the Wabash Cannonball,
and the bird on your shoulder
was speckled if you recall.
And when you hear a howdee
coming in a loud pitch.
You'll find Minnie and Roy
in a place called Grinder's Switch.
Now, Lord, there'll be more coming.
and it may not be too long,
I know you too get lonesome
for a good ole country song.
So if you want to be entertained
and make heaven a delight,
then let them angels pull up a chair
there's a show come Saturday night.

THE LINE

This is to all of those
who stood outside in line,
men, women and children
people of all kind.
Through rain and snow and heat
you stood faithfully,
hoping for a ticket
to get inside of me.
We tried our best to hold
each and every one of you,
but peeking through the door
was all some got to do.
Here's hoping that each of you
finally entered in,
this is to those who stood in line
for truly you are my friend.

VITO PELLETTIERI

Vito Pellettieri you got them on
when their spot was due,
then you got them off
when their part was through
They'd all still be running around
and wondering what to do,
I don't believe we would have made it
if it hadn't been for you.

OH ROY

"What a beautiful thought I'm thinking"
oh Roy, you gave me such a chill,
"concerning the Great Speckled Bird"
Roy I still get that thrill.
You put a hum in every heart
every man, woman, boy and girl,
you put a sound that someday
would be heard around the world.

Roy Acuff, Grandpa Jones and Boxcar Willie

OLD PICTURES

I was turning through the pages
of my old photograph book,
they're yellow with the ages
these old pictures that I took.
There's one of Bill Monroe
in his old straw hat,
and there's the old Martha White Show
with Earl Scruggs and Lester Flatt.
There's Jean Shepherd counting time
with her hands behind her back,
and the Fruit Jar Drinkers all in line,
Cousin Jody with an old tow sack.
Stony Mountain Cloggers dancing
Charlie Louvin on the phone,
the Willis Brothers prancing
Dolly doing her first song.
Billy Grammer with his first guitar
George Hay blowing that old fog horn,
Red Foley sitting in his old car
Johnny Cash, the day his son was born.
Pictures that go back for years
that bring back memory to my mind,
pictures of all those smiles and tears
that past years left behind.
They're torn and cracked, and corners gone
but they mean so much to me,
I know I'll never be alone
they'll always keep me company.

Early Opry on Fatherland Street

OUT FRONT

Professors have searched for the answer,
wise men looked in books of all kind.
"What makes country music so special?"
"How has it withstood the test of time?"

Professors say it's because it's earthy,
wise men say ignorance is to blame,
books say it's the Nashville sound
that brought country music its fame.
Perhaps some of these are the answer
but, professors forgot one thing in their plan,
I guess wise men just can't see it
but, we know it's the country music fan.
A fan's seen the Opry several times in a lifetime
with the exception of a few who dream that dream,
a fan's got a scrapbook of pictures and clippings,
and a bushel of autographs in between.
Girls will giggle at their favorite,
men will just stop and stare,
women will say, "honey, hug my husband
he's in love with you, but I don't care."
A fan can sing you every hit in country music
'cause every hit is on the shelf,
he's spread his music to other people
just by being his proud country self.
The loyalty to us is un-dying
he's seen us through hard days and nights,
the fan's in love with country music
and that love comes across the footlights.
So professor there's an answer to your question,
wise men you can stop your long hunt,
I'll help you put your finger on it,
in fact, put ten 'cause it's out front!

Hank Williams

Duke of Paducah

HANK

Aristotle talked to wisemen
and Plato did the same.
There was a man I listened to
Hank Williams was his name.

He spoke no fancy words about,
no lecture did he give.
He was a third grade dropout,
yet, degree in life he lived.

He walked among the common man.
He saw life through their eyes.
He knew the sound of laughter,
knew more the sound of cries.

Time swept him away in his youth,
but left us a history.
Aristotle talked to wisemen,
Hank Williams spoke to me.

THE DUKE

The Duke of Paducah
used to come in now and then,
but had to go to the wagon
cause his shoes was killing him.

YEP, THAT'S
HANK WILLIAMS' KID

Hank, a boy stood in your shadow
a few short years ago.
People watched to catch a glimpse
of you in his show.
He sang "Cheating Heart" and "Jambalaya"
just the way you did,
and everybody looked and said
Yep, that's Hank Williams' kid.
He'd do your recitations
and tear our hearts into,
Luke the drifter lives again
the way you used to do.
Then Hank, the boy grew up
and became his own man,
and he's one of the best
he's even got his own band.
He puts on a country show
that brings people to their feet,
He fills the auditoriums
there's not one empty seat.
He's in the spotlight on his own
and doing his own thing,
And I reckon he does a few
that Hank, you'd never sing.
Oh, he still does your old songs
they're still in the show,
People always ask for them
wherever he may go.
He may even go down a legend
just the way you did.
But with all that talent, people say
Yep, that's Hank Williams' kid.

Ryman Auditorium

LET HER GO, BOYS

"For many years they've stood on her stage,
watched the curtain go up and come down
now that the old Ryman is showing her age
they won't be coming around."

Well, the last show had just finished
and the crowd cleared out,
I found myself sitting in the auditorium
and a great silence fell about.
And suddenly I heard a voice
though no one I could see,
but somehow I sensed the Old Ryman
was trying to talk to me.

"Well Opry, my time has about come
they say I've seen my day,
they've put it in the paper
the children will go away.
Now they're gonna have a new home
it's going to be bigger and the best,
and as soon as it's finished
I'll be laid to rest.

Oh, they've tried to fix me up
but my age shows through I know.
They've tried to lift me face
for the biggest network show.
But no matter how they dress me up,
I'd still look the same.
Why, they even took away Ryman
and gave me a new name.

But it don't do no good
they're just wasting powder and paint.
After all you can't make an old girl
be something that she ain't.

Now, they say they're gonna move my stage
cause that's the vital part.
Guess I've come to a transplant
leave the soul but take the heart.

Oh, but listen to me go on
why the stories that I hold
and the memories that I've made
can't be bought with gold.
And don't be surprised after you've gone
if you hear sounds coming from my wall.
Why, I'll be shouting "Howdee"
and singing "Wabash Cannonball."

Lord, I've loved everyone
from the least to the biggest star.
And some of them have forgotten me
but they know who they are.
They say the new place will hold more people
I've stacked them in here until my sides would grunt
And I've seen the time when there was as many backstage
as there were sitting out front.

Now there have been words written about me before
and I'm sure there will be again.
I guess they'll be trying to make it easier
as I near the end.
Well, I'm getting sleepy now
I'd better say goodnight,
there's just one more thing
before I turn out the light.

You know, I used to hear, 'Let Her Go, Boys'
and they were talking about you, Opry.
Tonight they're saying 'Let Her Go, Boys'
and they are talking about me."

Opry House

MESSAGE TO OPRY HOUSE
FROM RYAN

Well, hello there, new Opry House,
Ole Opry speaking here.
There's a few things you ought to know
so you'd better lend an ear.
You're gonna have my children now
Lord, they can be a sight.
So I'll let you in on a few things
so things will go just right.

You'll have to watch Bill Carlisle
he gets to jumping now and then.
Porter don't take time to eat
and he gets to looking thin.

Justin will always leave early
for his midnight show.
And remember at Christmas time
Roy gets a new yo-yo.

Faron might get a little loud
and need calming down.
Box Car Willie is the happiest
when some old trains's around.
Connie will sing an old hymn
and bring a lump to your throat.
Dottie West is bad
about drinking too much Coke.

Minnie will tell the same old jokes
and bring the house down.
Johnny Cash loves to dress in black
when he goes to town.
Hank Snow will want rhinestones
all over his stage suits.
And it's hard to get Grandpa
to take off his old boots.

Tom T. will tell you stories
Jan Howard will make you cry.
Teddy will leave for Hollywood
and forget to tell you bye.
George Jones spends too much money
on things he wants to own.
Loretta Lynn's awful bad
about inviting everyone home.

Lonzo and Oscar will kid around
and look an awful sight.
Oswald takes longer getting to the mike.
Willma Lee will walk around
And give everyone hugs.
And you'd better like Bluegrass
for the sake of Ricky Skaggs and Earl Scruggs.

Monroe will sing higher
than a farmer calling hogs.
Skeeter Davis will bring home
all stray cats and dogs.
Jim always looks better
with Jesse at his side.
Oh yes, you may be surprised
when you meet Charlie Pride.

Now it would be impossible
for me to mention everyone.
You'll have to get use
to the way they go and come.
Besides, if I told you everything
I'd be out of breath.
There's just some things you'll have
to find out for yourself.

Now just another moment
then I'll let you go.
But there's a few more important things
I think you ought to know.
The children seem to stick together
that's always been their creed.
You'll find that when one is cut
they all tend to bleed.

And remember, they all have their fans
the fans made them what they are.
And there'll be those who'll
want to meet their favorite star.
This is something that will never change
and it won't change with age.
So try to take as many
as you can backstage.

Well, I'd better go now.
I've rambled on too long.
Be good to them, they'll be good to you,
and they'll love their new home.

Kitty Wells and Jim Reeves

I BET THAT WAS YOU

I heard there was a man
dressed in Duckhead overalls.
And everywhere he went
he sang Eddy's "Cattle Call."
He said the Tennessee Plowboy
was the best he ever knew.
He had all of Eddy's recods,
why, I bet that was you.

And I heard there was a woman,
a better mother you couldn't find.
She rocked her babies every night
humming "You Are My Sunshine."
No telling how many miles she rocked
or verses she went through.
She's still got that old rocking chair,
why, I bet that was you.

And there was a blind boy
who used to sit and stare,
and listen to his favorite song
"Star Spangled Banner Waving Somewhere."
He'd of fought in a minute
of his ole Red, White and Blue.
He dreamed to be a soldier,
why, I bet that was you.

And there were couples by the thousands
who sat by their radio.
They had to get the dial just right
to pick up the Grand Ole Opry show.
They'd sit and watch the fire for hours
'til the last song was through.
Then they'd climb in that old feather bed,
why, I bet that was you.

Grant Turner

Ralph Emery

GRANT TURNER

Grant, I reckon you've
outlasted them all.
Among the announcers
you've always stood tall.
You got me through trying times
when others let me down,
and now after all these years
you're still a comin' round.
Maybe down deep you wanted to sing
and that's why you're here.
Grant, I heard you sing one night
and I'm glad you're talking, dear.
But I love you just as much
as I do anyone
and remember that I'll always
be proud to call you Son.

RALPH EMERY

You've promoted my children
all through the night.
When others were sleeping
you saw the early light.
You've gone beyond duty
you did it on your own,
You're one of the main reasons
this ole Opry's grown.

Wilburn Brothers

COUNTRY GIRLS

Dolly Parton and Barbara Mandrell
took me to Hollywood,
But we came home to Tennessee
like good country girls should.

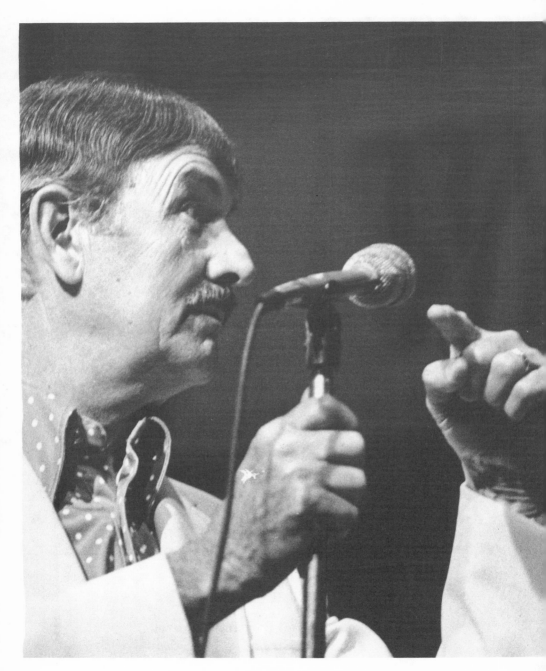

Archie Campbell

PRINCE ALBERT SHOW

That big advertising agency
up in big Chicago,
sent down big producers
to the Prince Albert Show.
Now they had big directors
pointing left and right,
telling everybody where to stand
and where to put the light.
Now we'd always done it simple
kinda feel as you go,
but, they had a big script
for the Prince Albert Show.
So all us country folks
couldn't find our place,
and we sure didn't know
which way we should face.
We were running into each other
and forgetting all our lines,
that big director kept waving
but we couldn't see the signs.
So we took that big producer
aside after the show,
told him Prince Albert could stay
but you boys got to go.
So they packed up their bags
and we eased their fears,
they never came back to Nashville
but Prince Albert stayed 25 years.

Jimmy C. Newman

THE BUS

When you see a painted bus
driving down the highway,
it's probably one of the children
and another show to play.
They use to drive cars
and I worried about them
all packed in like sardines
and tires lookin' thin.
They'd drive a long way
and sleep very little,
then someone else would drive
usually the one in the middle.
But they've traded in their cars
and got buses where they stay,
and sleep a little while
until another show to play.

JIMMIE ROGERS

It was in Meridian, Mississippi
a singer made the news,
and the world got a new sound
when Jimmie sang the blues.
He sang about the freight trains
and about the Brakeman's shoes,
all the people listened
when Jimmie sang the Blues.
My family looked up to him
he was the greatest in their views,
this world's a better place
cause Jimmie sang the Blues.

Tom T. Hall

OLD RADIO

That old upright radio
that connected with the wire
brought me into your living room
and I watched you watch the fire.

BEHIND THE SCENES

There are lots of people
you never see their name,
they aren't on the show
so they never get the fame.
But they work the Opry
as hard as anyone,
putting in long hours
before the show's begun.
They make sure the lights
are always on the dot,
and make sure the mikes
are always on the spot.
They sell tickets and soft drinks
and hand programs out,
without all of them
the show would be in doubt.
So thanks to all of those
who keep the show on air,
you give up your Saturday night
because you really care.

Marty Robbins

Porter Wagoner

DeFORD BAILEY

DeFord Bailey used to play
his harmonica every Saturday night.
He had to stand on a box
so he could reach the mike.
Four feet tall from head to toe
but packed with dynamite.
DeFord I can see you now,
still trying to reach the mike.

CITY SLICKER

Hey you big city slicker writer,
wrote about my Ryman in your magazine.
Said it was the ugliest place
that you'd ever seen.
Said the pews were held together
with old two by fours.
And it had tobacco juice stains
all over the old floors.
Said backstage was a nightmare;
said junk was everywhere.
And it was shaped like a big old toad
protruding in the air.
Well slicker, when you talk about old Ryman,
you're talking about me.
Thank God you're in Georgia
and I'm in Tennessee.

Wilma Lee and Stoney Cooper

Del Reeves

Connie Smith

Bill Anderson

Patty Loveless   Ricky Van Shelton

Randy Travis   Reba McEntire

NEWEST ONES

Lorrie Morgan, your daddy's proud
to see you in the light,
before he left this world
he passed you the mike.
Patty Loveless, I cried the night
Teddy gave you the guitar,
a promise he made long ago
before you became a star.
Randy Travis, you remind me of Hank
the way you stand on stage,
Mel McDaniel, "Your Baby's Blue Jeans"
caused a country rage.
Ricky Van Shelton, keep on your cowboy boots and hat
you'll always please your fans,
Holly Dunn, never let go of your "Daddy's Hands."
Reba McEntire, you rode 'em high
when you were in the rodeo,
now you ride 'em high
on the Grand Ole Opry show.
Riders In the Sky, cowboys will always live
as long as you're around,
you brought in the western song
when you came to town.
Like the others, you'll be legends
like the ones that's gone before,
if you'll just keep the faith
and open every door.

Lorrie Morgan

Riders In The Sky

Mel McDaniel

Holly Dunn

Stringbean

ELVIS

Elvis played the Opry
on October 2nd, 1954,
Blue Moon of Kentucky
was like it never was before.

CARNEGIE HALL

In 1962 Merle, Flatt and Scruggs
played Carnegie Hall.
New York went country
they say it was a ball.

Earl Scruggs and Lester Flatt

Johnny Russell

Chet Atkins

Johnny Cash

Johnny Wright   Kitty Wells

COUNTRY MUSIC HALL OF FAME

I was in the Country Music Hall of Fame
down on Music Row,
they had collected everything
even Roy's old yo-yo.
There were guitar straps
and cowboy hats
all down the hall,
cowboy suits and cowgirl boots
and posters on the wall.
They had Patsy Cline's pretty dress
and old papers with Opry news,
there were old hand fans
and past programs
and sheet music with the blues.
There were matching guitars of the Wilburns
and costumes around the bend,
there were old Ryman pews
Ralph Sloan's dancing shoes
a road atlas of Loretta Lynn.
There was a tux of Charlie Pride's
and Pop Stoneman's autoharp,
there was Carl Smith's belt
an old hat of felt
and one of the girl's scarfs.
I left the memories all teared up
and heart so proud it swelled,
and as I left the museum room
an old Wurlitzer played Kitty Wells.

Jeannie Seeley, Dottie West and Jan Howard

President Nixon

President Reagan

PRESIDENTS

The Presidents of the United States
are coming to see me,
that's a sight I never thought
this ole girl would see.
An if you don't believe
they've walked upon my stage,
the proof is in the pictures
that you see on the page.
Would you believe country music
would ever go that far,
imagine we're in the White House
a long way from Tootie's Bar.
Those gone on before never knew
just how far we'd go,
keep it close to the ground
was the Solemn Old Judge's motto.
That's what we've done all these years
I'm a close to the ground girl,
I guess that's why Ole Orpy is heard around the world.

OPRY AIN'T NO POET

I know what you're thinking
Ole Opry ain't no poet.
But just had a few things to say
And took this way to show it.

*Through my doors have passed
the heartbeat of this country.
Thank you,
love and until.*

*Ole
Opry*

ACKNOWLEDGEMENT PAGE

To Minnie Pearl,
who has always been
an Ambassador of Country Music,
for taking time to read and acknowledge this book.

Thanks to the Grand Ole Opry,
Jerry Strobel and his office
for all the help and assistance they have given.

Thanks to Joe Horton,
Nashville historic photographer,
who supplied pictures.

Thanks to *The Banner* and *The Tennessean*
for use of Country Music pictures.

ABOUT THE AUTHOR

Margaret Britton Vaughn, known as Maggi, was born in Murfreesboro, Tennessee, but grew up in Gulfport, Mississippi. She is one of the Grand Ole Opry's greatest fans. Her love for Tennessee and Country Music brought her back to Nashville in 1965. Besides having songs recored by Loretta Lynn, Ernest Tubb, Conway Twitty and others, she is also a poet and playwright.

Maggi found a great satisfaction in writing this book. When asked why, Maggi replied, "I've written about what millions like myself grew up on!"

Maggi has reached down and touched the heart and soul of "Ole Opry." Ole Opry comes to life and relives her years of memories. She wrote this for the Country Music fan – after all, that's why the Grand Ole Opry has celebrated all these birthdays.

Maggi is Poet Laureate of Tennessee and resides in Bell Buckle, Tennessee.

ABOUT THE BOOK

In 1975, *The Tennessean* published Maggi Vaughn's book <u>50 Years of Saturday Nights</u>. The book celebrated the Grand Ole Opry's 50th anniversary. Since that time, many people have asked Maggi to update the book and reprint it. Maggi has updated, revised and captured all the years of the Grand Ole Opry show. Our thanks go out to *The Tennessean* and John Seigenthaler for the reprint rights of this book.

The Bell Buckle Press hopes
you have enjoyed this book.
If you would like extra copies for friends,
please send $9.95
plus $1.25 for handling and postage
to
Bell Buckle Press
P.O. Box 486
Bell Buckle, Tennessee 37020.

Thanks for your patronage.

Autographs